PrayerStarters

On the Way to Forgiveness

Text © 2000 by Denis Robinson, O.S.B.
Published by One Caring Place
Abbey Press
St. Meinrad, Indiana 47577

Library of Congress Catalog Number
00-100740

ISBN 0-87029-340-0

Printed in the United States of America

PrayerStarters

On the Way
to Forgiveness

by Denis Robinson, O.S.B.

ONE
CARING
PLACE

Abbey Press

Introduction

It is one of the lamentable facts of life that we have all had the experience of being hurt by the words or actions of others. It is also true that we know that through our own cruel or careless deeds and speech, we have hurt others. The anger and pain that comes from having our feelings hurt or disregarded can be devastating and sometimes long lasting. In our hearts we know that there is no true peace in life until we are AT PEACE with our neighbors, our friends, and the members of our families.

Yet we go on, year in and year out, persisting in our pain, desperately in need of healing old grudges and wounds. This book may be just the tool to help us take the first step toward forgiving others or seeking forgiveness. These prayer starters are a road map to a happier life free from past heartaches and grievances. By going deep within ourselves we can find true peace and joy in reveling in God's love, a love always ready, even anxious, to forgive. May these words and musings help you on that journey.

"God does not change what is in people, until they change what is in themselves."
—The Koran

Jubilee

"On the year of jubilee you will have the trumpet sounded throughout all your land."
—Leviticus 25:2

The ancient Hebrew people believed in the celebration of jubilees, times when slates were wiped clean, when financial ledgers were balanced and those who were burdened with debt given a new start.

All of us need a jubilee now and then. We need a time in our lives when we can say, "I am sorry" and a time when we can say, "You are forgiven." There might be tense relationships in families, between friends or neighbors. There might be old hurts and pains that need to be cured. We may even need to be reconciled with the past, with memories, with ourselves, or with God. Is this the time for a jubilee? Certainly!

PrayerStarters

In what ways can I celebrate forgiveness?

Lord, open my heart to the spirit of celebration! Give me generosity of mind and soul that I might do what is necessary to seek the fullness of life in you.

Deep Within

*"O Lord my God, I cried to you for help
and you have healed me!"*
—Psalm 30:2

The most difficult step on the road to healing and forgiving past afflictions, grudges, and grief is the first step. We must embark by going deep within ourselves. In our hearts, in the silent recesses of our minds and imaginations is the secret place where memories are preserved, grudges nourished, and anger grows. It is sometimes exhausting, almost impossible, to look within and name hostility, injury, and disquieting memories.

PrayerStarters

How can I look within and be honest with myself about my anxiety, my hurts, my pains and disappointments?

Dear God,
    Give me the grit and power to face the events I hold in the buried parts of my heart. Give me the energy to be fearless in searching my memory and being honest and up front about what has injured or caused me pain in the past. I know I can do this with your help, with your love, with the support that you give me.

Growing Up and Growing Down

*"I utter my complaint and I moan
and he will hear my voice"*
—Psalm 55:17

There is a little story about a man who wanted to build a tower up to heaven in order to talk to God. When he sought advice about the best way to do this, he was told by a sage to get a shovel. The man ignored what he considered half-witted advice and started to build the tower anyway, which promptly collapsed. He returned to the sage who repeated his earlier advice, adding the words: "If you want to build a high tower to heaven, then you have to dig a deep foundation."

PrayerStarters

Loving God,

Listen to my voice as I seek you deep in my own soul. Comfort and guide me on the path to forgiveness, healing, and growth—a path that I realize may bring me to the depths of who I am. Help me to understand that the sorrow of the realities I might face within myself can be healed and strengthened by your loving presence.

Touching the Wounds

"Do not forsake me when my strength is spent."
—Psalm 71:9

When I was a child we had a Christmas tradition. We had a little plaster statue of the baby Jesus that we placed under our Christmas tree each year. We loved our little Jesus doll and took good care of him. He was an important part of our lives. Then one year, tragedy struck. Our dog, in a particularly aggressive mood, decided to play with Jesus and tore his little plaster leg from his body. The family was so upset. We did not know what to do with this broken, mangled Jesus. Should we throw him away? Should we try to repair him? In the end we decided to leave him as he was, broken and wounded. Somehow he seemed to be Jesus even more that way.

PrayerStarters

How do I face my own "woundedness"? Do I nurse wounds so that they cannot heal or do I face my "woundedness," seeking healing for my loss and pain to grow beyond loss to wholeness?

Dear God,
   Help me to know that even in the midst of my wounds, you can show me what it means to be whole. Help me to accept your own wounded presence in my life.

One True Word

"Lord, lead me in your truth."
—Psalm 25:5

Ernest Hemingway once said that his goal as a novelist was to write just one true sentence. But sometimes the truth is not easy for us to face. And sometimes we hide from it like adults playing hide and seek with children: We know where they are hidden but we pretend for the sake of the game. So often in our dealings with others we hide from the truth and say: "I am not angry" or "That did not hurt me." Inside, we know the truth is different because it is betrayed in every shying eye and sharp-turned word. Relationships wither in the chill of lies like naked blossoms assaulted by first frost, and we are dishonest with others and ourselves and say nothing is the matter.

PrayerStarters

Lord, what is needed is the truth, an honest reckoning of accounts. Help me to be honest.

Because of this incident in my life, I feel like this:

Write some of those things here.

_____

_____

_____

Facing Facts

*"I will hear what the Lord God will speak
for He will speak peace to his people."*
—Psalm 85:8

We all grew up with the axiom that "honesty is the best policy." Why, then, is honesty often so hard? We know that there are just some parts of our lives that we want to keep hidden from others, from God, and even from ourselves. We begin to develop clever lies about our lives. We say we are not hurt when we are really devastated. We claim to have forgiven others when we still hold grudges. Healing and forgiveness can never take place in our lives as long as we are unwilling to admit that we are in need of them. Today is the day to face facts. Of course, this can be so rough. We have become too comfortable with the cover-up.

PrayerStarters

God, I know that I can never be cured if I do not admit that I am hurting. I know that I can never find or seek forgiveness if I will not acknowledge the injury. I need your help, God, to be honest and truthful with myself and others. I seek your face, O God, and your truth. Amen.

In heartfelt honesty, with God at your side, write down in a journal some of the truths of your life that you have tried to evade because their memory is too aching. God is with you.

Facing Grace

"Lord, teach me your way."
—Psalm 27:11

If being candid and true with ourselves compels us to face the facts about our lives and the reality of our relationships with others, it also forces us, as people of faith, to face the fact of God's grace at work. We know the anguish of life and we know its raptures, the chill of loss, and the thrill of new discoveries. If we know these things, we must also know that it is the love of God that sustains us through times of trial and days of joy. Grace is that serious intuition that we are not alone, even when we feel most separated from others and from ourselves. Grace is the impulse that leads us to reconciliation, to forgiveness, because it springs from the overwhelming generosity of God.

PrayerStarters

Today, notice the evidence of God's constant grace:

In the power of nature

In the foibles of others

In the rushing beat of my own heart

O God, I am alive and it is your miracle that sustains me and encourages me on life's often perilous highway. I know I can face whatever life offers with your help and your constant presence.

The Faults of Others

"O Lord, you have searched me and know me."
—Psalm 139:1

How is it possible for us to begin to forgive others, perhaps for bitter, devastating things they have done or said to us? What if we could begin by seeing others and ourselves for who we truly are: flawed and broken people. We have only to look around, to see the secret pain in the faces of those around us, the tear-filled eyes, the determined chin. So many of us spend our years wearing masks of courage to hide our real feelings, our vulnerability, and our interior turmoil. Could it be true that our "enemies" and those who have hurt us could, for all their bravado and seeming courage, be really broken children, selfish and afraid in their hearts? Could it be so with me?

PrayerStarters

God, help me to see with an inner vision. Help me to see beyond facades and masks to the inner world of those I know. Help me to find there the flawed beauty of those in need of renewal and wholeness. O God, help me to know my own flaws, the hidden places that I try to hide from others and myself, and from you.

You might now look at the twenty-fifth chapter of the book of Proverbs.

The Frailties of Others

*"He has pity on the weak and the needy
and saves the lives of the needy."*
—Psalm 72:13

We have all used or heard the time-worn expression, "Achilles' heal." We know it refers to our soft spots, those aspects of our personality or make-up that are vulnerable to the attack of sharp words, actions, or attitudes. People have a knack for finding the soft spots in others and using that realization to injure, to intimidate, or to isolate other people. We know we have weaknesses, some that we try very hard to hide from others. There are secret places within ourselves we like to keep private and we are shocked when these darkened recesses are exposed to the light of day by someone else's careless revelation.

PrayerStarters

Is it possible that the suffering we have experienced at the hands of others might well stem from their own vulnerability and insecurity? We react in hateful ways when we are hurt.

Lord, help me to see the pain of others, even pain that they may want to hide. Help me to understand that "woundedness" sometimes prompts wounding. Is it possible to clothe me in your boundless sympathy?

Anger at Others

"Refrain from anger and forsake wrath.
Do not fret, it only leads to evil."
—Psalm 37:8

We all value our reputations and our good names.
We spend our whole lives cultivating the good opinion
of others through our behavior and our words. We are
rightly devastated when our reputations and our integri-
ty is called into question. Mean-spirited gossip, thought-
less conversations in the lunchroom at work, or an idle,
unthinking word can destroy what we have so careful-
ly built. We become angry with those who have hurt us.
Hostility and resentment at others can be deep and
long-lasting. We hold grudges. We hang on to some
injuries and slights even years after the initial sting has
faded away.

PrayerStarters

Lord, help me to understand the bitterness and resentment I may harbor against my friends, my co-workers, my neighbors, or my family members.

Perhaps today is the day to take an inventory of my REAL feelings:

About my family members
About my neighbors
About my friends
About my co-workers

Anger at Ourselves

"The Lord is my strength and my might."
—Psalm 118:14

One of the real dangers of hostility and resentment is turning that anger on ourselves. Sometimes when others have bruised our egos or betrayed us, we might begin to feel that it is our fault, that we are less-than-adequate friends, spouses, children, or parents. There is nothing more deadly than self-loathing. It eats away at self-esteem, tranquillity and productivity. God did not mean for us to live this way. Jesus said to his disciples, "I came that you might have life in the full." We are all made by the loving Creator as wonderful in our own right. We might do some things that are wrong, but God still loves us. How can we fail to love what God loves, even ourselves?

PrayerStarters

Are there events in my life for which I need to forgive myself?

Have I wrongly ascribed the guilt of others to my own fault and weakness?

God, help me to understand anger I may have toward myself. Help me to overcome feelings of shame and inadequacy. Touch my life today with the reassurance of your presence, of your acceptance, and your wonder.

Anger at God

"Hear my voice O God in my complaint."
—Psalm 64:1

There are times when we might be angry with God. This is often the hardest anger to admit. It is not rare to blame God at times for things that happen to us: the loss of a loved one or friend, a failed relationship. The Psalmist was frequently irate and frustrated with God. He had questions and complaints for God. He did not always understand or appreciate God's ways.

We frequently deny anger and go through life as though everything is fine. Can God understand my anger? Can God understand even when I feel angry with Him? Of course He can. God is compassionate with our anger because He loves us so intensely.

PrayerStarters

God, have I been angry with you? Bewildered, broken-hearted, or in pain? I know, loving God, that I can tell you about my feelings at all times. If I am angry even with you, I know you will always respond with love and patience.

Healing the Myth of Perfection

"The Law of the Lord is perfect."
—Psalm 19:7

Television and movies may seduce us into believing that life can be flawless and beautiful, yet we know that real life is not a sit-com or a romantic movie. In life we have to deal with real blemishes, dandruff, less-than-perfect homes, and cranky friends and family members. While the Law of the Lord is perfect, at times that law is written with convoluted lines. In spite of this truth some of us still expect perfection, sometimes missing the imperfect graces that life has to offer.

PrayerStarters

God, help me to see the glory of imperfection, the wonder of missed opportunities, the grace of human weakness, my own and that of others.

Healing the Myth of Happiness

"In the shadow of your wings I take refuge
till the storms of destruction pass by."
—Psalm 56:2

Another myth with which we frequently struggle is the persistent myth of happiness. Many times we are led to believe that we are supposed to be happy and fulfilled all of the time. Of course, this is a problem because our vision of happiness and success might be skewed or we fail to realize that all real rewards come with real costs. We can only be truly fulfilled when we realize that struggle and striving are also a natural part of life and can be as life-giving as "Easy Street"

PrayerStarters

Lord, help me to embrace my struggles and disappointments as something that will lead me farther down the road of life to true fulfillment and understanding of your will in my life.

Healing Memories

*"By the rivers of Babylon—there we sat down and there
we wept when we remembered Zion."*
—Psalm 137:1

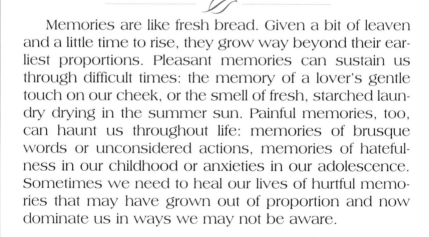

Memories are like fresh bread. Given a bit of leaven
and a little time to rise, they grow way beyond their ear-
liest proportions. Pleasant memories can sustain us
through difficult times: the memory of a lover's gentle
touch on our cheek, or the smell of fresh, starched laun-
dry drying in the summer sun. Painful memories, too,
can haunt us throughout life: memories of brusque
words or unconsidered actions, memories of hateful-
ness in our childhood or anxieties in our adolescence.
Sometimes we need to heal our lives of hurtful memories that may have grown out of proportion and now
dominate us in ways we may not be aware.

PrayerStarters

What is my most vivid friendly memory of childhood?

What is a hurtful memory that I would like to forget? Write it on a piece of paper and tear it to pieces.

God, you know all our memories and thoughts. Help me to heal the memories of pain and disappointment and revel in the memories of fondness and celebration.

Growing in Adversity

"Turn to me and be gracious to me,
give your strength to your servant."
—Psalm 86:16

How many people do you know who go through life, not really paying attention, not really living? Certainly all of us get bogged down at times in trivialities, in meaningless pursuits, and even in wrongdoing. Sometimes, though, we can lose our way through real adversities that we face, the sickness and death of a loved one, our own illness, financial difficulties, or broken relationships. There are real troubles in life. How do we face them? Could it be that the pains we have suffered, even at the hands of others, could be opportunities for growth and for maturity?

PrayerStarters

Name in a silent time with God some of the real adversities you have suffered in your life.

How have these crises been stifling to your relationship with God or with others?

How have they been opportunities for enrichment of strength and faith?

Dear God, no life is without trials and devastation. Help me to see beyond the blinding rush of pain to the clear assurance of new birth and love.

Growing Personally

"Lead me in your truth and teach me."
—Psalm 25:5

You do not need this little book to tell you that life is a journey. Sometimes the journey is smooth sailing. Sometimes the way is a bit more jagged. It is never colorless. You also do not need this little book to tell you that some of the most momentous experiences of life are the stormy ones. Growing pains are a part of life, but there is no growth without change and a little discomfort. So often, however, we try to minimize this aspect of life by covering up adversity with drugs, alcohol, or inappropriate relationships. To live fully is to face hardship. To face hardship is to grow and mature. The question is not a life without trouble but rather a life in which we courageously face trouble and doubt.

PrayerStarters

What are my goals for personal growth?

How do these goals involve healing past rifts with others?

O, my God, I call to you for help. Teach me your ways!

Growing in Relationships

"A true friend sticks closer than one's nearest relative."
—Proverbs 18:24

Relationships are complex. In the history of a friendship, a romance, or a marriage, there are moments of tender intimacy and serious betrayal. Doubt and confidence walk hand-in-hand. Our friends, our loved ones, are our source of greatest comfort. They are also the very ones that can wound us the most. We may feel estranged from close relatives, yet know real and lasting intimacy with our friends. One thing is certain, however: relationships advance in the crucible of adversity. True intimacy is cultivated in times of shared trials and need. Can we use this insight to help us understand the need to forgive others, to use times of hurt, doubt, and even betrayal to grow to a more full life?

PrayerStarters

Who is your oldest friend?

How has your friendship been forged in the furnace of difficult times and pain?

Is there need for healing in this friendship? Are there unspoken apologies to be offered or accepted?

Loving God, you are our friend. Help us to know that passion and suffering may be our way to genuineness and tenderness as they were for your Son, Jesus.

Expect the Expected

*"Let me hear of your steadfast love in the morning,
for in you I put my trust."*
—Psalm 143:8

We might like to think of our lives as fascinating and full of escapades, but most of us are faced each morning with the daily round of routines. Most days are like every other, filled with joys and laughter as well as little disappointments.

We somehow believe that God is not God unless there is drama, thunder, smoke, the crashing of waves. Yet God is not always in the earthquake, but rather the still, small whisper. We must be attuned to God's little invitations for healing and forgiveness every day.

PrayerStarters

God, help me to see the chances I have every day for an excellent and more perfect life. I know you speak to me in the daily routine of my life, in my housework, in my errands, in the office.

Knowing God's Will

"Lord let me know your ways."
—Psalm 25:4

People frequently seek the advice of their pastors because they are having difficulty discerning God's will in their lives. What does God really want me to do with my life? Should I consider marriage, children, the single life, or a religious vocation? Does God want me to consider a new career path or a change in residence? Sometimes it can be difficult to sort out these perplexing questions, even when we are sincere in our desire.

PrayerStarters

Dear God,

Sometimes, it seems, your will is mysterious. Help me to see the times when I know what you intend and yet I avoid it. Help me to embrace your way of forgiveness, even when I'm unsure how to go about it.

Confounding Nature

*"He made the storm be still and the waves
of the sea were crushed."*
—Psalm 107:29

God is the creator of all things, including our human
nature, so raw and naked, so sleek and radiant as it is.

So often we think or hear in the face of human moral
or physical frailty and thoughtlessness: "O so and so is
all too human." Perhaps the truth is that sometimes we
are not human enough. God has the power to modulate
our natures, weak and poor as they can be, and forge
them more like his own; good, forgiving, "transforma-
tive" in themselves.

PrayerStarters

What are the ways in which I would like to change?

How would I like for God to heal splintered aspects of my personality and life?

What would I like for God to do for others?

Guilt and Shame

"O Lord, pardon my guilt."
—Psalm 25:11

Mulling over past bruises and insults often leads to feelings of guilt and shame. Guilt is that part of my understanding that comprehends that I have done something wrong. Guilt convicts us and keeps our consciences on the right course. Shame is different. Shame is pernicious and ruinous. It robs us of life by turning the "rightness" of guilt to self-loathing. If we fail to acknowledge our wrongdoing (and we know when we are wrong) then we can begin to believe that we are bad people. Or worse, we can try to convince ourselves that those who have wronged us are bad people. The source of guilt must be faced and eradicated for shame to be subdued.

PrayerStarters

Lord, help me to face the reality of my guilt when I have wronged others. Help me also to be released from useless feelings of shame that can only stifle my relationships with others and with you.

Moving to Forgiveness

"For everything there is a season."
—Ecclesiastes 3:1

There is nothing more certain than the seasons. The frigid beauty of winter is the seed-ground for the verdant exuberance of spring. The excess of spring gives way to the sweltering reality of summers that decay into the chromatic astonishment of autumn. It is also true of the seasons of our lives that one time gives way to another. Sometimes we realize without prompting that the time has arrived for action. This is the season to put away old grievances, to seek forgiveness, and to forgive. The coldness of our grudges and grievances must give rise to new life, a life that can only spring forth by forgiving the faults and frailties of others and ourselves.

PrayerStarters

Lord God, teach me in the ways of nature to put aside the wintry season of my life, a season of bareness and bone-chilling cold, and to seek the warmth of spring. Help me to move to forgive those who have harmed me and to forgive myself. Most of all help me to understand that your love sustains me in times of transition and doubt. Lord, I am tired of the hurt. I seek a new season.

Forgiving Ourselves

"I will get up and go to my father."
—Luke 15:18

Without a doubt, one of the most beautiful images of forgiveness and reconciliation in the Bible is the story of the prodigal child in Luke's Gospel, the familiar story of the "problem child" who decides to turn the tide of his fortunes and seek reconciliation with his family.

In some ways we are all problem children. Haven't we all transgressed, missed the mark, or had too much confidence in our ability to do it our own way? Likewise we all reach a turning point in life, a moment of truth when we decide that forgiving or seeking forgiveness is better than bitterness and grudges. Life is too short to wallow in the pigsties of guilt and depression.

PrayerStarters

Revisit the story of the prodigal child in Luke 15:11-32.

Lord, help me to turn away from the dead-ends of grudges, shame, and fear. Help me to take the first step to forgive others or seek forgiveness. I know this is not an easy road, God. I also know that you will be with me as I walk home to love and reconciliation.

Forgiving Others

*"While he was still far off, the father saw him
and had compassion; he ran and put his arms
around him and kissed him."*

—Luke 15:20

The character of the father in the parable of the prodigal child is rich. Luke unveils for us in this parable the exquisite image of the father who runs out to greet his son, even though the boy has proved an ungrateful wretch.

The question for us in this whole drama for forgiveness and reconciliation is: How do we respond to those who seek forgiveness from us? If we are in need of forgiveness in our lives, from others, and from God, certainly we must learn to first be skilled at forgiving.

PrayerStarters

Forgiving God, help us to be like you. Teach us to forgive others with a generous heart and an open will. Train us to be swift in mercy and slow in judgment. Reconciling God, be our guide; for your steps are sure while ours often falter.

Forgiving God

"His elder brother was in the fields."
—Luke 15:25

The third character in this little play is in many ways the most troubling. The older brother refuses to have anything to do with the celebration initiated by his younger sibling's homecoming. The problem for us, of course, is that there are times when we can relate to this young man's dilemma. He has done everything lawfully. He has not dishonored his father, his family, or his legacy and yet he is not receiving any attention.

Often we can become jealous of the generosity which God seems to show toward others, particularly those we might not view as model citizens or disciples. Can we learn to forgive God for being so generous?

PrayerStarters

God, help me to embrace your generosity. May I somehow, even falteringly, learn to imitate it.

Forgiving the Community

"Rescue me, God, from my foes."
—Luke 58:2

Sometimes the anger we experience in our lives is anger toward others, toward God, or toward ourselves. Sometimes it is anger toward the community. Are there things in my culture, in society, or in my own neighborhood toward which I harbor ill feelings? Do I feel I have been wronged by some injustice or sin that is greater than any single act? Many people feel harmed by the prejudices, the lack of fairness, or the competitiveness of the environment in which they live. Do we need healing on this larger scale?

PrayerStarters

Dear God,

Help me to touch my anger and pain I may be feeling at the injustices of my culture or my society.

Help me to challenge wrongs where appropriate and accept the things in life I cannot change.

Moving to Forgetfulness

"In the days to come all will have been long forgotten."
—Ecclesiastes 2:16

We all know the old adage, "Forgive and forget." We also know that nothing is that simple, but certainly the motivation to forgive and reconcile involves something more: the desire to put the past in the past. How open are we to forget past transgressions? Do we still hang on, nursing our wounds even when forgiveness has been sought and granted?

Likewise, we do not wish to fall victim to what we might call "doormat syndrome." That is conveying the belief to others that we are easy marks, that we can be treated in any way whatsoever and always "forgive and forget." Actions have consequences, but candid and forgiving hearts yield consequences as well.

PrayerStarters

Loving God, you have created us as such amazing, intricate creatures. Help us to search our motives and our desires. Help us to truly learn to put the past where it belongs. Help us mostly to be accountable for what we say and do.

Mourning and Moving On

"Depart from evil and do good so you shall abide forever."
—Psalm 37:27

Life is filled with choices. Many of them are inconsequential, almost meaningless: What kind of soap should I buy this week? Others are more important: Should I get married or not to this person? Nevertheless, all choices involve some sacrifice. If I choose this road, I must forget about these possibilities. Every choice is also a loss. Sometimes we must learn to acknowledge and move beyond these losses.

What do we lose when we make the choice for forgiveness and reconciliation? We lose our old hurts, our grudges, and our fears. Ironically, sometimes we have become so accustomed to living in the pain and suffering that we may not know how to live without them.

PrayerStarters

Do I depend upon my own misery? How can I depart from mourning and misery and activate the goodness and the example of God within me?

Do not forsake me O Lord; O my God do not be far from me; make haste to help me O God of my salvation.
—Psalm 38:21-22

Reconciliation

"Create in me a clean heart."
—Psalm 51:10

Reconciliation is more that just the ability to forgive and forget. It involves something positive, something proactive. Reconciliation implies creating a clean heart and forging new opportunities in relationships. If we believe that growth is tempered by adversity and that times of pain and doubt can help yield new harvests, we must uncover the good, even in past hurts. Reconciliation means not only moving beyond, but also moving toward.

PrayerStarters

What are the opportunities for growth in my experience of forgiving someone close to me?

How can I employ the wisdom of having been forgiven to change my life, to realize a new opportunity?

Lord, you are the God of fresh starts and new beginnings. Help us to see the season for conversion in every act of reconciliation.

A Cause for Jubilee

"Now is the acceptable time. Now is the day of salvation."
—Second Corinthians 6:2

These short meditations on the need for forgiveness and reconciliation in our lives have brought us full circle to the celebration of jubilee. Jubilee happens when we wake up one morning and realize that our lives could be so much happier and more fulfilling if we only did a little housecleaning. Jubilee happens, when at the end of the day our reflections encourage us to open our hearts to the needs and hurts of others and seek peace. Why should we continue living in sorrow and misery when happiness is only a step, a word, a letter, or a phone call away? When should we open ourselves to the life God intends for us? Now is the acceptable time. Now is the day of salvation. Today is jubilee!

PrayerStarters

Lord, help me to take the first step today toward a new and freer life. Help me to trust you, to trust others, and to trust myself to become happier and more whole. Amen!

About the Author

Denis Robinson, O.S.B., is a monk of Saint Meinrad Archabbey in southern Indiana. He serves as Director of the Continuing Education program at Saint Meinrad School of Theology, and teaches courses in systematic theology. Fr. Denis also gives retreats around the United States.

PrayerStarters Series

- *PrayerStarters for Dealing With Anger.* #20099
- *PrayerStarters When You're Worried.* #20098
- *PrayerStarters on the Way to Forgiveness.* #20101
- *PrayerStarters in Times of Sadness or Depression.* #20100
- *PrayerStarters in Times of Pain or Illness.* #20110
- *PrayerStarters to Help You Handle Stress.* #20107
- *PrayerStarters for Busy People.* #20109
- *PrayerStarters to Help You Heal After Loss.* #20108

Available at your favorite bookstore or gift shop, or directly from:
One Caring Place, Abbey Press,
St. Meinrad, IN 47577
(800) 325-2511
www.onecaringplace.com